Wheels of Justice
Washington State Bicycle Accident Law

By Christopher M. Davis
Attorney at Law

Table Of Contents

Chapter One
Accidents Happen 4

Chapter Two
The Law Is Not What You See On Television 8

Chapter Three
You've Been In An Accident: What Now? 10

Chapter Four
How Do You Know You Have A Case? 20

Chapter Five
Bicycle Law 24

Chapter Six
Bicycles And Children 34

Chapter Seven
Insurance 39

Chapter Eight
The Litigation Process 62

Chapter Nine
The Advantages Of Hiring A Lawyer 74

Chapter Ten
Important Resources 81

About the Author 83

Chapter One: Accidents Happen

It's a sad fact that every year in the United States there are about 900 bicycle accident deaths. Adolescents between the age of 15-19 and adults 40 years and older have the highest bicycle death rates, according to the Centers for Disease Control and Prevention (CDC).1 Emergency rooms saw 494,000 bicycle-related injuries in 2013.2 Intersections are particularly dangerous, accounting for 35% of bicycle accidents.3 These accidents not only affect people's lives, but take a toll on the economy in general. Injuries and deaths from bicycle accidents alone cost approximately $10 billion in 2010.[4]

These statistics are frightening. Despite decades of work to make cycling safer, the reform of traffic laws, improvements in intersection and crossing design, the raising of public awareness, and the introduction of such innovations as bike lanes and bike boxes that have made Washington, according to the League of American Bicyclists, the most "Bicycle Friendly State,"[5] accidents happen much too often.

Though we travel on them every day, few people realize how complicated and hazardous roads can be. There are all kinds of dangers that we have to look out for all the time. A moment's inattention or distraction can turn a pleasant cycle ride on a quiet street into a terrible tragedy that can end in a lifetime of pain or even the death of a loved one. This is

1. http://www.cdc.gov/motorvehiclesafety/bicycle/
2. http://blogs.consumerreports.org/safety/2010/03/bike-fatalities-hold-steady-while-deaths-from-atvs-drop.html
3. http://www.walkinginfo.org/pedsafe/crashstats.cfm, NHTSA
4. http://www.nsc.org/news_resources/injury_and_death_statistics/Pages/EstimatingtheCostsofUnintentionalInjuries.aspx
5. http://www.wsdot.wa.gov/News/2009/05/26_BicyclingFriendlyState.htm

particularly true in the case of children, who are often not aware of the dangers of playing near traffic.

The reasons for these incidents are many. One major cause is distracted driving. Motor vehicles are dangerous instruments that require constant alertness; even an experienced professional driver can find it impossible to react in time to every situation. A driver who divides his or her attention between driving and doing something else greatly increases the risk of a serious accident. These distractions can be something simple like eating a hamburger, tuning the radio, or adjusting the air conditioning. Modern technology adds even more distractions, such as operating a GPS unit while driving, using a cell phone without a hands-free device, or even texting. Alcohol is also a major factor. Drinking alcohol reduces reaction time, clouds judgment, and impairs concentration. Another cause is speeding. Driving too fast is always dangerous. A driver can only react so fast and a vehicle can only brake so quickly. Going over the speed limit makes it only harder to stop in time. In slippery conditions, it also increases the chances of skidding out of control. Speeding on crowded urban roads where people may step off the curb unexpectedly can literally be fatal. Like speeding, generally poor and reckless driving puts cyclists at risk. Safety depends in part on being able to predict the actions of others and reckless behavior such as running stop signs, tailgating, failing to signal turns, and improper lane changes can make it difficult for cyclists or other drivers to react properly.

Weather can also be hazardous. Rain, snow, and fog can reduce visibility, and wet or icy road surfaces can be extremely slippery. In such conditions, even the best drivers may have difficulty and it is very easy to underestimate how challenging it is to keep a vehicle under control. Any of the above causes are made worse by driving at night when visibility drops dramatically and the danger of impaired vision from oncoming headlights is added. Even the most careful driver under the best conditions must be alert when the sun goes down–especially when suddenly encountering a cyclist who is wearing dark clothing without the proper reflective equipment. Combine these hazards and their causes with the laws surrounding bicycle accidents, and it may not be easy to determine who is legally at fault. Many people think that because they've been hit by a car, they have an open and shut case. Not so. A determination of liability is heavily dependent on the facts involved in each individual case. Since the driver and bicyclist each have a duty to act "reasonably under the circumstances," the parties may share fault for what has happened. In these cases, it may take much more effort, time and expense by the victim to recover fair compensation for his or her medical bills, lost wages, and other damages caused by the accident.

But if you're the accident victim, the injuries are usually much more severe than the typical personal injury case. You will likely experience the trauma of an emergency room visit. You may have had a prolonged stay in the hospital or face months of reconstructive surgery or physical therapy. Perhaps you're struggling to pay off medical bills that just keep coming and pile up as time goes on. There's a very good chance that the accident has caused you to miss work and your income has been affected so that you're having trouble making ends meet. You might have suffered a significant loss of mobility and may be physically unable to perform activities of daily living. Emotionally, you may be struggling as well, since depression is a common symptom following a traumatic injury. Then you discover that your insurance company isn't as helpful as it should be. You may suspect that they aren't telling you everything. The amount they're willing to pay may not be anywhere near what you need to keep your head above water. How can this be? There can't be anything more straightforward than getting knocked off your bike by a car. Why are things suddenly so complicated and why can't you get the compensation you need and deserve? How did things suddenly become so complicated and confusing? What are the next steps you should take?

Sadly, the reason for all of this is that the legal process after an accident isn't as simple as many people think. Far from being cut and dried, the justice system has many gray areas and procedural traps. And the laws regarding bicycle accidents are very complicated. What seems obvious at the scene of the accident may not be so easy to prove years later in a courtroom. If everything isn't fully documented, witnesses not interviewed, or medical treatments are not properly followed, then achieving a successful outcome in your case can be very difficult. Insurance companies often intentionally deny, delay and defend against these types of legitimate claims to increase profits. They know how to use the complexity of the legal process in their favor. After you've been in an accident, you should be concentrating on getting better, not dealing with uncooperative insurance companies through confusing, unfamiliar rules and procedures. This is why you shouldn't try to do this alone. You should engage the services of a knowledgeable and experienced attorney to help protect your interests—especially when the damages are high and the injuries are severe. Your attorney will determine whether or not you have a case, help you gather and organize the materials needed to pursue it, and handle negotiations with the insurance company and other parties to get the best result possible.

Chapter Two: The Law Is Not What You See On Television

Many people get their knowledge about the world from watching television. People see fictional doctors and they think they know how medicine works. They see fictional police officers and think they know how law enforcement works. And they see fictional lawyers and think they know how the law works. Unfortunately, the law is not the same as what you see on television. The purpose of television drama is to entertain. It's supposed to catch our attention and hold it through the next commercial break. It isn't intended to give an accurate picture of how lawyers and courts really work. Because of this, television creates various myths about the law that confuse many people the first time they step into an attorney's office.

Law Is Not Dramatic

Television gives the impression that lawyers spend their days rushing from courtroom to courtroom making dramatic speeches, and that most cases are suspenseful battles before juries. Often, these cases will end with some dramatic surprise at the last minute that reveals the truth. In fact, most legal work is very routine; the resolution of cases depends on the experience and judgment of your attorney rather than dramatics. As part of the litigation process, most of the evidence is shared between the attorneys of the parties involved, so there is little room for surprises, which usually do more harm than good anyway.

Most Cases Are Settled Out of Court

On television, most cases are settled in court before a jury, but in reality, very few personal injury cases go to trial. Trials are risky, expensive, complicated, and slow. So most cases are settled through a process of negotiation that does not involve a jury. In Washington State, more than 95% of personal injury cases are settled out of court.

Litigation Is Extremely Slow

Television law moves very quickly because the story needs to entertain the audience. The client retains a lawyer, the case goes to trial, and everything is resolved in the same episode. In real life, the justice system is very slow. Trials are scheduled far in advance and take at least 18 to 24 months in most cases before they're even heard by a jury. Personal injury cases often take longer because most cases aren't resolved until the person is finished with his or her medical treatments or has reached the maximum level of improvement, which can take several years.

It Isn't All DNA Tests

Forensic science is very visual and makes for very dramatic television. That's why it shows up so often in legal dramas. Unfortunately, this leads people to think that courts routinely use all sorts of sophisticated scientific tests in every case. In fact, such tests aren't used nearly as often as television implies because they are time consuming, expensive, and not very reliable except under certain circumstances. In real life, most cases don't rely on DNA and exotic lasers. They use the standard techniques of evidence, witness testimony, records, photographs, and the attorney's experience and knowledge of the law.

Chapter Three: You've Been in an Accident: What Now?

Being injured in an accident is often a traumatic experience, and all it takes is a moment of inattention on the part of a motorist. Each year in the United States, an estimated 900 cyclists are killed in collisions with automobiles. Because cyclists are often difficult for motorists to see and lack the protection of metal cars and airbags, those who are fortunate to survive a collision often suffer severe injuries and permanent disabilities that can require years of expensive medical treatment and rehabilitation. Despite every reasonable precaution, accidents still happen. When they do, it's important to take the right steps to ensure that you preserve your claim and increase the likelihood of achieving a successful outcome. That's why in many cases, hiring an experienced attorney to represent your interests is one of the smartest decisions you can make.

The First Step

The first thing to do is to STAY CALM. Right after an accident, your body is filled with adrenaline. You may be very frightened, angry, or both—and your instinct may be to confront the driver of the vehicle. This is a natural and perfectly understandable response, but don't. The best thing that you can do is to keep your temper in check and stay calm. You need to get information about the driver of the vehicle, witnesses, other parties that may be involved, and the accident scene itself. If you waste your energy with anger, you will not be able to focus on what you have to do, and it will be difficult to get the people at the accident scene to cooperate with you. If you are injured, getting upset may make you unaware of how severe your injuries are and cause you to neglect them or fail to seek professional medical attention.

Gathering complete information is important because even though insurance companies are legally obligated to compensate the victim, they will often go to great lengths to deny the claim or minimize the amount of compensation they have to pay. Most people who enter the claims process are surprised to learn how far insurance companies will go to delay, deny, or minimize a claim. As a result, you need to make sure that you have as much reliable information about the accident and your injuries as possible. This will strengthen your claim and increase the odds of a favorable outcome.

It's also important to get as much information as possible at the time of the accident, because it may be months or even years before a case is resolved. In most cases involving injuries, you should always call the police so that an investigation is done. The police officer will usually take witness statements and gather information that you or your attorney will need later on. You need to remember that what may seem perfectly obvious to you about what happened won't be so obvious to a court or a jury many months or even years in the future. There is also the possibility that you may not notice an injury or damage to your property until it's too late to show that the accident was the cause of the injury or damage—unless you have already collected the evidence. Worse, the accident scene can change, physical evidence at the scene can disappear, injuries can heal, witnesses can forget or become hard to track down, and your recollections of events can start to fade. In fact, one danger for the victim of an accident is post-traumatic amnesia (PTA), which may result in the victim having no memory of the events either leading up to or immediately after the accident.[6] In cases of PTA, getting full information about the accident in order to resolve a settlement is vital, because the victim may be unable to say what happened with any confidence–if he or she even remembers it at all. In such cases, witness testimony is particularly important, since the victim cannot give a full account.

The Next Steps

The first people to contact after an accident are the police, by calling 911. If someone has suffered a serious injury, the 911 dispatcher will notify the police and also arrange for emergency medical services. Police reports are very important for resolving a claim, so make sure that the officer who responds files one. If for some reason an officer does not respond, file an accident report at the local police or sheriff's office within 72 hours of the accident.

Pitfalls: Ten Mistakes to Avoid

If you are the victim of a bicycle accident, you have the legal right to recover compensation for your injuries and damages. However, the insurance company will go to great lengths to deny the claim or minimize the amount of compensation it has to pay. As a result, there are certain steps that you should take to protect your rights and increase your chances of a successful recovery. Or put another way, there are at least ten mistakes that you should avoid. Committing one or more of these mistakes can have devastating consequences in your legal claim and/or significantly reduce the amount of compensation you may recover.

6. Shaw, N.A. (2002) "The Neurophysiology of Concussion." Progress in Neurobiology 67 (4): 281–344. doi:10.1016/S0301-0082(02)00018-7. PMID 12207973.

1. **Not calling the police.** If you have had an accident, the proper authorities should be notified immediately. An investigation by the authorities can produce information and witness statements in the police report that may be critical in helping you establish liability against the vehicle driver or other parties involved in the accident.

2. **Failing to seek medical treatment promptly.** If your injuries are serious enough to warrant medical attention, then you need to consult with a doctor promptly, or go to your local emergency room. Insurance companies may refuse to believe that the injury is serious unless prompt medical attention has been received. Also, a visit to the doctor will create a chart note that becomes a permanent record in the case. The magnitude of your injuries, as well as your symptoms, will be recorded by a professional, and this information can be used later to prove the extent of your injury. Also remember to complete all your treatments. Failure to do so may not only jeopardize your health, but your case as well.

3. **Failing to take multiple photographs of your injuries and wounds.** This is extremely important. Often, the value of an injury is heavily dependent on its initial appearance, along with the appearance of subsequent disfigurement and scarring that develops over time. You should take multiple photographs over the period of time that it takes your injuries to heal. Insurance companies will often put a great deal of weight on photographs; especially if the injury is significant and any subsequent scar or disfigurement is severe. We have all heard the adage, "A picture is worth

a thousand words." This is particularly true with photographs that depict severe injuries, disfiguring wounds, or prominent scars.

4. **Giving a recorded statement to the other driver's insurance company.** The at-fault driver's insurance company will almost always ask you for a recorded statement. Don't do it! The statement will be used by the company to look for any "holes" in your story. There are always minor discrepancies when a person is asked to recount a traumatic incident. The carrier knows this and will use these either to reject your claim entirely or to minimize the amount of compensation it has to pay out. The only reason to give a statement is to help the insurance company. Sometimes it may be beneficial to give a statement to the company, but you should always consult with an attorney first to determine if that situation applies to your case.

5. **Signing insurance company forms and medical authorizations.** For the same reasons you should not give a recorded statement to the insurance company, you should not sign any forms or medical authorizations that it requests. Again, these forms are used to protect the carrier's interest. The insurance company will be looking for any information in your past medical history to build its case against you. In one case of mine, the client had executed medical authorizations allowing the company to dig far back into her medical history. These records revealed unflattering information about my client to the extent that the information damaged her reputation and made it difficult for me to settle the case for a much higher amount. Please don't help the insurance company by

signing documents it asks you to sign before you have consulted with a lawyer.

6. **Failing to document everything.** You should write a statement about the incident while everything is fresh in your mind. Your claim may take many months, or even years, to resolve. Writing things down will help you to record and recall important facts that may be useful later on. Take complete photographs of the accident scene including signs, signals, the vehicles involved, skid marks, and your injuries. All of these are very important because accident scenes, especially intersections, can change over time. Reference points change, skid marks disappear, and even signs and signals can be altered, so it is vital that the appearance of the scene at the time of the accident is preserved. Because camera phones are now so common, be sure to ask witnesses if any of them recorded the event. It's possible that someone has it on video. Photograph the damage to your bicycle and then take your bicycle to a reputable bike shop. Have them inspect it and record any damage caused to your bicycle by the accident. Remember to keep calm while doing all of this and do not confront the vehicle driver.

You should keep a file to store documents, photographs, and records related to the claim, like the vehicle driver's insurance information, address, telephone number and license plate number; receipts; medical records; names and phone numbers of witnesses; correspondence from the insurance company; police reports; bicycle repair bills; etc. If you decide to hire a lawyer, your file of records and documents can provide enormous assistance to the attorney and his or her staff in representing your interests.

7. **Settling your claim too soon or appearing too eager to settle your claim.** If your injuries are severe, it may take many months or years before your injuries heal or before they reach maximum improvement. The insurance company will likely want to pressure you into making a quick settlement. Don't! The carrier knows that quick settlements mean much lower pay-outs. And if you have experienced any disfigurement, scarring, or loss of function, it may take a long time before the doctors know whether it is permanent or whether future revision surgery may be necessary. The existence of permanent scars, disfigurement, or disability can dramatically increase the value of your claim, so you are always wise to wait to resolve your claim.

Also, if you appear too eager to settle the claim, this can negatively impact the case. Insurance adjustors are trained to look for signs that may weaken your negotiating position. If you are in debt or need money fast, the insurance company will use this fact to its advantage by making much lower settlement offers than might otherwise be warranted. In one case of mine, the client had tried to negotiate a settlement on his own. But during negotiations he also revealed that he had substantial debt and needed the money fast. When I got into the case, the insurance adjustor used this information against me to keep the settlement unreasonably low. The client ultimately had to accept this unreasonably low offer because the insurance adjustor knew that filing a lawsuit would delay resolution of the claim for at least another 18 months. The insurance adjustor knows that a person who really needs the money fast is in a much weaker position to ask for a higher settlement. Therefore, don't appear too eager to settle. Take your time. In fact, be willing to negotiate the claim over a period of days or even weeks. Patience is usually met with a much higher settlement figure.

8. **Not being absolutely honest with your doctors and the authorities.** Your credibility as a victim is extremely important. Oftentimes an incident or claim can only be proven based on what the victim says and what the vehicle driver says. Thus, if you give statements to your doctors or the authorities that turn out to be false, this will likely cause severe damage to your case or destroy it completely.

Although it sounds like a cliché, honesty is absolutely the best policy. Be above reproach when it comes to describing what happened in the incident and how the injuries have affected you. Even minor exaggerations or incomplete versions of the incident you tell to the doctor can cause major problems in the claim. Also, be aware that statements you make to others can be used against you. If you make a false statement to someone like a witness or co-worker or friend, that person can be used as a witness against you. So being honest to everyone is the best policy.

9. **Failing to hire a lawyer.** If your injuries are serious or permanent, then it is usually in your best interest to hire a lawyer to help you resolve the claim. Typically, more serious injuries mean higher damages, which means a

higher value of the claim. When there's more money at stake, the carrier will typically fight harder to avoid paying out a fair settlement. Please remember that insurance companies go to great lengths to train their adjustors on how to dig up information to use against you and then teach them how to use this information to negotiate and minimize your claim. Adjustors usually handle thousands of claims every year, so they are expert negotiators and evaluators of injury claims. Many times, the insurance company will assign an accident case to the person who has the most knowledge and experience with these types of claims. So that adjustor will be well-versed on the law and understand the defenses and arguments available in a bicycle accident case. In most cases involving severe injury or scarring, the experienced accident lawyer will be able to obtain much more compensation than the unrepresented victim can recover on their own. Studies show that this is even true after a lawyer subtracts attorney's fees. I handle bicycle cases on a contingency fee basis, so there is no out-of-pocket cost to see me and I can usually tell you whether the case is worth pursuing with a lawyer or if you can handle it on your own.

10. **Using social media to talk about your claim.** With the increasing popularity of social media, more and more people are disclosing highly personal and private facts and circumstances about their lives on the Internet. This is a dangerous practice when it comes to protecting the value of your case. Most insurance companies now will diligently search social media sites like Facebook, Twitter, and Instagram to look for any information about you or your case. Even what appears to be

harmless or innocent information can be successfully used against you to either defeat the case entirely or significantly reduce the claim's overall value.

WARNING: By attempting to settle your claim on your own, you incur the risk that you might do or say something that might permanently damage the case in some way. Even if you hire a lawyer later on, that lawyer is pretty much stuck with whatever has happened in the case to that point. If you make statements that contradict the medical records, or say something to the adjustor that reveals what amount you are willing to accept as a settlement, or seek out inappropriate treatment, this can make it virtually impossible for the lawyer to resolve your case for maximum value. Oftentimes the best thing accident victims can do is to hire counsel immediately to act on their behalf. This helps to ensure that no mistakes are made and that everything is handled professionally, so the chances of recovering a satisfactory settlement are maximized.

Chapter Four: How Do You Know You Have a Case?

Generally, you will only have a legal right to recover compensation if your injuries were caused by another party's negligence. In Washington, the term "negligence" is defined as a person's failure to exercise "ordinary care" or the kind of care that is necessary in the particular situation that led to your injury. Not only can a person be found negligent, but so can a corporation or governmental agency.

Oftentimes it is easy to determine whether a party was negligent, such as when a driver runs a stop sign. The violation of a known rule, statute, or regulation can also provide evidence of a party's negligence. For example, if a person injures you and also breaks the law while doing so, that violation may be admissible in a subsequent trial to prove that the person was negligent.

Comparative Fault

Sometimes there may be more than one negligent party who has caused harm. Washington follows the law of comparative negligence (also called comparative fault). This means that more than one party may be responsible for damages due to negligence. For example, let's say Party A and Party B both negligently injured you and that the damages were calculated at $100,000. Party A was found 25% responsible and Party B, 75%. Party A's share of the damages is $25,000 and Party B's share is $75,000. Under the law of comparative fault, each negligent party is only responsible for its share of damages as determined by the jury–or a judge, if the matter is tried without a jury.

Joint and Several Liability

In Washington, there is an exception to the rule of "comparative fault." This occurs when the injured person is considered fault-free, or when it is determined that the injured person is not at fault. In that situation, if there are multiple negligent parties who have caused the injury, each of them will be jointly and severally liable for all damages. This means that each negligent party is responsible not only for their respective share of fault, but is also individually responsible for 100% of the damages. Take the example of Party A and Party B above. If joint and several liability exists, then Party A will be responsible not only for its proportionate share of $25,000 but also for the full amount of damages calculated at $100,000. This holds true for Party B, who will be responsible not just for its proportionate share of $75,000 but also for the full $100,000 award. The purpose of the law of joint and several liability is to fully compensate an innocent victim even if it means that a negligent defendant may have to pay more than their share of fault for causing the accident.

Negligence of the Victim

Washington's law of comparative negligence means that the proportionate share of fault of all potential negligent parties must be considered, even if it involves the conduct of the victim. This means that as the victim, you can be held negligent and therefore wholly or partially responsible for your injuries and damages. In Washington, the issue of your degree of negligence may also be called "contributory negligence."

Statute of Limitations

The statute of limitations is the period of time during which a legal action must be started. In Washington State, the limit for starting personal injury cases is three years. But that does not mean you should wait three years to resolve your claim or file a lawsuit. As time passes, evidence can be lost or destroyed. The scene of the accident often changes, records can be erased or lost, witnesses' memories can fade over time, and important witnesses may be difficult to locate. Generally, the more time that passes, the greater the likelihood that important evidence may be lost or destroyed. Simply put, waiting too long to investigate and/or prosecute the claim in court may cause irreparable damage to the case.

WARNING: It is a dangerous practice to wait until the statute of limitations period is about to expire before filing a personal injury lawsuit. If the lawsuit is filed right before the deadline and if the defendant cannot be found, or if the wrong defendant is served, the case will be dismissed and the injured person gets nothing. For this reason, it is very important to hire an attorney long before the statute of limitations expires. Many attorneys will refuse to accept a case when the statute of limitations period is about to expire because there may be insufficient time to investigate the case, file a lawsuit, and locate and personally serve the proper defendants. The lesson: do not wait until the statute of limitations is about to expire before you protect your rights.

Claims Against a Government Entity

If you have a claim against a governmental entity, such as a town, municipality, county, or state, certain requirements must be met. A verified claim form must be served on the authorized agent for the governmental entity. Serving a valid claim form on the government is a prerequisite to bringing a legal case against the government. The name and address of the authorized agent who can accept service of the claim form is required to be kept as a matter of public record with the auditor in the county in which the entity is located. With claims against the state of Washington, the agent who is authorized to accept service of the claim form is the state's Division of Risk Management in Olympia, Washington. To be valid, the claim form must contain certain information, including a description of the conduct and circumstances that brought about the injury or damage, a description of the injury or damage, the time and place the injury or damage occurred, the names of all persons involved, the residence of the claimant for a period of six months immediately before the claim arose, and a statement of the amount of damages claimed.

It is important to note that the content and service of the claim form must substantially comply with the requirements of the statute. Failure to comply substantially may result in the claim being denied and/or dismissed by a court of law. Once a claim form has been properly verified, presented, and served on the appropriate governmental entity, you must wait a period of 60 days before a lawsuit can be filed in court. The failure to wait 60 days is a fatal mistake that will invalidate the claim and result in the dismissal of the case. The filing and presenting of claims against a governmental entity can be complex and confusing, so you are wise to consult with or retain an attorney as soon as possible following the accident.

Chapter Five: Bicycle Law

As people become more environmentally conscious and health conscious, we see more and more bicycles on the road every day, particularly in Washington. Bicycles are not only becoming more popular for exercise or recreation, but also for transportation between home and work. In Washington State, our government and many local communities are encouraging people to switch from motor vehicles to bicycles. As more bicycle lanes and paths are built, especially in cities like Seattle, more accidents are likely to happen. It's therefore very important for both drivers and cyclists to understand the law as it applies to bicycles.

What Is a Bicycle?

Bicycles are familiar objects and we all know one when we see it, but to prevent confusion, Washington State law defines a bicycle as a device propelled only by human power with two wheels in tandem, one of which is at least sixteen inches in diameter. "Bicycle" can also apply to unicycles and pedal-powered tricycles with wheels that are at least twenty inches in diameter.[7]

Negligence

Bicycle cases are often not black and white when it comes to determining who was responsible or if an accident was truly caused by someone's negligence. Since both the driver and bicyclist can be held responsible for the cause of an accident, the facts in each case must be examined meticulously. For example, just because a cyclist is hit while in a crosswalk does not automatically mean that the driver was 100 percent at fault.

---

7. RCW 46.04.071

You need to know how the cyclist entered into the crosswalk, where the cyclist was on the roadway when hit, if the cyclist was easily visible, how fast the driver was going, and several other important factors. And the place to begin that determination is with the law.

The laws involving bicycles are very important because in order to win a claim, you must demonstrate that the motorist acted careless in some way, and that carelessness was a proximate cause of the accident. You can do this by showing that the motorist was driving too fast, not paying attention, or performing some other careless act which contributed to the accident. These laws, however, impose the same duty of care upon the bicyclist. This means that a cyclist who is hit while in a marked crosswalk can still be held negligent if that cyclist acted carelessly. For instance, the cyclist may share a degree of fault if he or she rode into the crosswalk without first watching for traffic, or if he or she attempted to cross at a time when it was impossible for the motorist to stop safely. In that situation, the cyclist may share a significant percentage of fault for causing the accident that inflicted him with injury.

For these reasons, educating yourself about local laws involving bicycles is very important for understanding not only the nature of your claim, but also the process that will allow you to resolve it. This is particularly important in Washington State, where the state government and many local communities in recent years have been very active in encouraging more people to travel by bicycle. Part of this promotion has involved changes in laws that favor cyclists, but which many people may not be fully aware of. In other words, knowledge of the law can help keep you and your loved ones safe.

Right of Way

The legal concept of "right of way" refers to the right one party has over another to proceed on the roadway. Oftentimes the right of way is spelled out explicitly by signs or signals that tell motorists and cyclists what to do. Under Washington State law, motorists and cyclists are required to obey all signs and traffic signals that are properly installed and in good working order. In situations where there are no signals or signs, such as an uncontrolled crossing or the middle of a block, the law spells out who has the right of way in that situation. However, factors such as visibility, the speed at which a bicycle is traveling, and the ability of the driver to react in time can affect the question of who has the right of way.

This is one of the reasons why having complete information about the accident is so important. Physical evidence, photographs, the position and conditions of signals, and eyewitness accounts go a long way toward showing who had the right of way, and these details can be vital to the outcome of a case. In many cases, a determination of which party had the right of way is the starting point to deciding which party is negligent for causing an accident.

Pedestrian Law and Bicycles

We usually think of a pedestrian as someone who travels on foot, but that isn't always the case. For example, under Washington State law, a bicycle riding on a sidewalk or in a crosswalk is legally regarded as a pedestrian, though when it's traveling along the road it's a vehicle and must obey the rules of the road like any other vehicle.

The most basic laws pertaining to pedestrians are the ones regarding right of way. Pedestrians have a nearly absolute right of way in the crosswalk at an uncontrolled crossing. "Crosswalk" in this case means that part of the road at an intersection area between the sidewalk on one side of the crossing to the other. If there is no sidewalk, then it's the area within ten feet of the intersection unless there's a marked crosswalk.[8] Of course, if the crossing has signs or signals, all pedestrians must obey them when crossing the street.

Due Care Always Required

A person's right of way is not infallible. Even the best designed roads and intersections require caution and judgment to remain safe. So, drivers and cyclists are expected to use due care at all times. Cars are large and fast-moving, while bicycles are often difficult to see. It isn't enough to know that you have the right of way over someone else. You have to remain constantly observant and be aware and conscious of what is going on around you at all times. If you ride in front of a speeding car on the grounds that you're "in the right," you could end up in the hospital (or worse) as well as discovering that you were negligent for causing the harm.

Driver Duties

The duty of a motorist towards bicyclists is at all times to exercise ordinary care, to remain observant, and to respect the right of way of others. This is particularly important if a driver sees a bicyclist who is a child or who is obviously confused or incapacitated. The driver must not only take all reasonable and proper precautions to avoid a collision, but also must give an adequate warning by blowing his or her horn.[9]

Stopping

Unless otherwise indicated by signals or signs, a driver approaching an intersection must yield to a cyclist in a crosswalk. The driver must slow to a complete stop and remain stopped so long as the cyclist is within one lane of the half of

---

8. RCW 46.04.160
9. SMC 11.58.310

the side of the road where the vehicle is either stopped or is going to turn.[10]

Signal Not in Operation

There are times when, owing to damage or power outages, a traffic signal stops operating. If this happens at an intersection and the signals aren't replaced by a temporary signal, policeman, or flagger, then the intersection is regarded as an uncontrolled four-way stop. When approaching an uncontrolled intersection, a driver must exercise due care to make sure that any cyclist in, or attempting to enter a crosswalk, is given the proper right of way.[11]

Emergency Vehicles

Though cyclists usually have the right of way at a crosswalk, they must yield to emergency vehicles, such as fire engines and ambulances, when these vehicles are using their lights and sirens. Cyclists must remain in a place of safety until the emergency vehicles have passed.[12]

Control Signals

If an intersection has signals or signs, then a cyclist must obey those instructions. This may seem obvious, but it is surprising how many people disregard signs and signals simply because they are riding a bicycle. Running a red light while riding a bicycle is just as dangerous as doing so in a car.[13]

Sidewalks

The presence of driveways, parking lots, garages, and loading docks means that vehicles often must drive over

---

10. WAC 132E-16-040
11. RCW 46.61.183
12. RCW 46.61.264
13. RCW 46.61.050

sidewalks to get to where they're going. Oftentimes the driver is backing up and has difficulty seeing where he or she is going. In this situation, the danger of colliding with a cyclist is very great, so the right of way of the cyclist is nearly absolute. The sidewalk is a place of safety, so drivers must yield.

Exceptions

Which is a bicycle, a vehicle or a pedestrian? The answer is: it depends on the circumstances. When a bicycle is traveling on the road, it is a vehicle and is treated as one under the law.[14] The rules of the road that apply to motor vehicles also apply to bicycles (though there are some exceptions) and cyclists are expected to obey those rules. Traffic lights and signs also apply to cyclists and must be obeyed as well.[15]

The main exception is when a bicycle is traveling along a sidewalk or using a crosswalk, it is regarded as a pedestrian under the law. In that situation, the same laws and rights of way apply to the bicyclist as to a person on foot. For example, the driver of a vehicle must yield to a bicycle on a sidewalk or in a crosswalk.[16]

With this in mind, the best way to understand the rights and obligations of the cyclist is not only to know the rules of the roads as they apply to vehicles, but also as they apply to pedestrians.

Because a bicycle can be treated both as a vehicle and a pedestrian under the law, we often find it in a legal gray area, filled with exceptions. These exceptions are important because they not only help in determining negligence in bicycle accident cases, but are also intended to increase bicycle safety. One example is the recent introduction of "bike boxes" at many

---

14. RCW 46.04.670
15. RCW 46.61.050
16. RCW 46.61.261

Seattle intersections to make bicycles more visible and allow them to go through the intersections before the motor vehicles.[17]

Bicycle Duties, and Motor Vehicle Duties Related to Bicycles

Closed Routes

Though bicycles enjoy the same rights as motor vehicles, there are exceptions to this with some routes in Washington State being closed to bicycles. Due to construction or because the route in question is too dangerous for bicycles to share with motor vehicles, the Washington State Department of Transportation keeps a list of closed routes with suggested alternatives where available. You can find this list on the Internet at http://www.wsdot.wa.gov/bike/Closed.htm. In addition, local municipalities may have their own restrictions as to where bicycles have access.[18]

Yielding to Pedestrians

When on a sidewalk or crossing, a bicycle is regarded as a pedestrian, but a bicycle traveling at speed is still a potentially dangerous machine that moves silently and can catch pedestrians unaware–especially when approaching from behind. The law therefore states that bicycles must yield the right of way to pedestrians.[19]

Riding at Night

As with other vehicles, the visibility of bicyclists is of major importance. Because of their narrow profile, bicycles are especially difficult to see at night. To make them more visible,

---

17. "Seattle gets 'bike box' to make street safer for cyclists," Seattle Times, September 29, 2010.
18. RCW 46.61.160
19. RCW 46.61.261

Washington State law requires bicycles to display a white front light that is visible from at least 500 feet way and a red rear reflector. For added protection, a red rear light may also be used along with a reflector.[20]

Riding on Shoulders vs. Bike Lanes

Bicycles are faster than pedestrians, but they are usually slower than motor vehicles, so bicycles are required to keep as far to the right-hand side of the road as is safe, unless making a left-hand turn or overtaking another vehicle. If a bicycle is traveling on a one-way street, the left-hand side of the road may be used as well. Bicycles may also use designated bike lanes and the shoulders of the road if they are available, but may also choose not to do so for reasons of safety.[21]

Riding Abreast

Since bicycles have a very narrow profile, they may ride two abreast on the road, but no more than that, provided they do not unnecessarily block traffic.[22] Riding abreast is the technical term for bicycles riding side-by-side in the same lane of a roadway.

Riding with Traffic

Because a bicycle is sometimes thought of as a pedestrian, some cyclists think that a bicycle is safest when it, like a pedestrian, travels on the left-hand side of the road toward oncoming traffic. In fact, the speed and poor visibility of a bicycle makes this extremely dangerous. This is particularly true at intersections where drivers don't expect bicycles to

---

20. RCW 46.61.780
21. RCW 46.61.770, RCW 46.61.425
22. RCW 46.61.770

approach on the left-hand side. Because of this, bicycles are required to travel in the same direction of traffic.[23]

Passing on the Right

Drivers are generally required to pass other vehicles on the left, but for bicycles this is usually impractical or unsafe. Washington State law provides for this by allowing bicycles to pass other vehicles on the right if there is enough room for bicycle traffic there.[24]

Car Doors

One of the most dangerous and most difficult to anticipate hazards facing bicyclists is the suddenly opening car door. The door of a parked car can open in an instant—too fast for a cyclist to react, and the resulting injuries can be severe or even fatal. A cyclist can minimize risk by staying alert and exercising due care, but the law requires that drivers must show particular caution when opening the doors of a vehicle until it is safe to do so, and they should also not leave doors open longer than needed to load or unload passengers.[25] Even though these accidents typically occur when a vehicle is not in motion, a driver can be held liable and financially responsible for a cyclist's injuries in these cases.

Helmet Laws

According to the National Highway Traffic Safety Administration (NHTSA), nearly 70% of all fatal bicycle crashes involve head injuries. The NHTSA also states that bicycle helmets are effective in preventing or mitigating head

---

23. RCW 46.61.770
24. RCW 46.61.115
25. RCW 46.61.620

and brain injuries as much as 88% of the time.[26] Yet in the United States there is no national bicycle helmet law nor does Washington State have one. However, some Washington municipalities have laws requiring bicycle helmets. The Washington State Department of Transportation maintains a list of these municipalities at:
http://www.wsdot.wa.gov/bike/helmets.htm.

---

26. http://www.nhtsa.gov/DOT/NHTSA/Communication%20&
%20Consumer%20Information/Articles/Associated
%20Files/810886.pdf

Chapter Six: Bicycles and Children

A Special Case

When it comes to road accidents, children are a special case. All parents have a moment of panic when their children start to cross the road without a guiding hand to keep them safe. We drill our children from an early age about how dangerous cars can be, we remind them of the importance of staying safe, and we work to make looking both ways into an unbreakable habit. However, despite all our efforts, children lack the same perspective as adults about the hazards of motor vehicles and roads in general. Never having operated a motor vehicle, children haven't yet developed the understanding of the weight and power of a car, the damage that one can do, and how long it takes to bring one to a full stop. Children oftentimes play near or on roads in residential neighborhoods. Roads and cars are so familiar to children that they accept their existence as natural. Children often fail to see roadways as potentially hazardous places. Children also live in a simple and ordered world where rules are rules. They believe a car can't hurt them because all drivers are supposed to stop, when in fact many do not. Children are also small and difficult to see and they sometimes dart into the road suddenly and without warning. If they are on bicycles, young children may have trouble controlling them. Add to this the fragility of children's still-growing bones and you have a particularly vulnerable group.

Then there is the question of responsibility. Under the law, the degree to which a child is responsible or partly responsible for an accident will depend on the child's age. The law states that children below the age of six cannot be held negligent because they are too young to understand what may be appropriate and careful behavior. Children age six and older can be held negligent, but only if they act in a manner that is careless when compared to another reasonable child of the same age.

By the same token, the degree to which parents are responsible for their children's actions depends on the circumstances and the acts involved. In some cases, parents may be immune from liability for their child's negligent acts. Known as the doctrine of "parental immunity," a parent cannot be held legally responsible for certain types of negligent acts by the child, such as the failure to adequately supervise a child. The law also states that a parent's liability for a child's dangerous acts is limited to "reckless" behavior, which is more serious than negligence. The term recklessness is typically defined under the law as willful and wanton behavior.

These are additional reasons why the advice of a knowledgeable and experienced personal injury attorney is so important in bicycle accidents. Cases involving children are not only far more tragic and distressing than those involving adults, but they can oftentimes become extremely complicated and enter into gray areas of the law that are impossible for the layperson to untangle.

Bicycles and Children

Bicycles are very much a part of childhood. In the United States, more than 70% of children ages 5 to 14 ride bicycles, and they ride 50% more than the average adult cyclist. With so many children riding bicycles, it's no surprise that many are involved in accidents with motor vehicles. Other than automobiles, bicycles are associated with more childhood injuries than any other consumer product. These incidents account for 21% of all bicycle-related deaths and nearly 50% of all bicycle-related injuries. That works out to 270,000 emergency room visits by children alone. Tragically, more than 130 children every year die in bicycle accidents. Nearly half of these children sustain traumatic brain injuries because of their failure to wear a helmet—or to wear a safe, properly fitted helmet.[27]

Studies have shown that a properly fitted bicycle helmet can reduce the risk of bicycle-related brain injuries by as much as 88%. Properly-fitted helmets can prevent an estimated 75% of fatal head injuries to children each year. Motor vehicles are involved in approximately 90% of the fatal bike crashes that happen each year. About 60% of child fatalities in bike-versus-auto crashes occur on residential streets. A child who does not wear a helmet is 14 times more likely to suffer a fatal crash than one who does. Clearly, the chances of injury and/or death decrease dramatically when a child wears a protective helmet while riding a bicycle.[28]

Children and Negligence

Washington State's law regarding comparative fault applies to children as well as adults. Like accidents involving adults, accidents involving children raise questions of negligence, where a child may be found partially at fault. For children, however, the negligence standard is defined much more narrowly. The law states that only children ages six and above can be found negligent. A child younger than six does not have the necessary mental development to know how to exercise ordinary care.

For children six and older, a child is negligent if he fails to exercise the ordinary care that a "reasonably careful child of the same age, intelligence, maturity, training, and experience" would exercise under the same or similar circumstances. This is an important distinction. It means that a seven-year old child cannot be judged according to the same standards that might

27. Safe Kids USA
    (http://www.safekids.org/assets/docs/ourwork/research/research-report-pedestrian-2005.pdf)
28. Bicycle Helmet Safety Institute (http://www.bhsi.org)

apply to a 12-year old child. The standard of negligence for children is also based heavily on the child's individual characteristics and traits. Conceivably, the actions of a special needs or mentally disabled child should only be judged based on the expected reasonable conduct by another child of the same age and/or intellectual capacity. The same goes for children who may be advanced or highly functioning. Highly-achieving children with excellent grades should only be judged based on the expected actions of other children similarly situated.

Parental Immunity

Usually, when a child has been injured in an accident, the conduct of the child's parents is called into question. Typically the insurance company will try to argue that the child was injured due to the parents' failure to adequately supervise the child. But this argument often fails because Washington State has adopted what is called the Parental Immunity Doctrine. Under this doctrine, a negligent parent is immune from liability for injuries caused to the child unless the parent was acting outside his or her parental capacity, or if the child's injuries were caused by a parent's willful and wanton misconduct. A parent is considered to be acting outside his or her parental capacity if the conduct is well beyond the bounds of appropriate parental parameters, such as conduct involving physical or sexual abuse. The Parental Immunity Doctrine is based upon the public policy of maintaining family tranquility and to avoid undermining parental authority.

An exception to the Parental Immunity Doctrine is when the child's injuries are due to a parent's negligent driving. That means a child is still permitted to pursue a legal claim against his or her parent if the injuries arose from a car accident that was caused by the parent. The doctrine also does not apply to those parents who engage in willful and wanton misconduct. Washington law has defined the phrase "willful and wanton misconduct" in this situation to mean the parent's intentional act or intentional failure to act in disregard of a known peril or hazard. This can be a difficult burden to prove. While the standard of negligence implies inadvertence or carelessness, the term willfulness suggests premeditation or formed intention in the face of known circumstances that would inform a reasonable parent of the highly dangerous nature of that conduct. Essentially, a parent's conduct must rise to the level of intentional or reckless conduct or extreme indifference that had a high likelihood to cause harm to the child.

Chapter Seven: Insurance

Dealing with the Insurance Company

In those cases where you have been injured by a negligent party who has insurance, you will at some point have to deal with the insurance company. You will need to address questions of liability and damages, including payment for past and future medical expenses and other damages incurred. This can be a daunting and unsatisfying task. You are likely already under a tremendous amount of stress in addition to the pain, suffering and disability caused by your injuries. Insurance adjustors are trained to take advantage of this fact so that the company can resolve or settle the claim as cheaply as possible.

First, a word about the insurance industry when it comes to resolving injury claims. It has been said that the moment a person has been injured by someone's negligence, that person has also entered into a war with the insurance industry. That is not an overstatement. For more than 30 years, the insurance industry has spent hundreds of millions, if not billions, of dollars on advertising to spread false and misleading information about accident claims. The industry wants people to believe that the justice system is out of control and that people who file lawsuits are getting millions of dollars for minor injuries.

Take it from someone "in the trenches" who has settled and litigated thousands of injury claims; such insurance industry propaganda simply isn't true. You will occasionally read in your local newspaper about a million-dollar settlement for what appears to be a minor injury. But a closer inspection of the evidence will usually reveal that the negligence was egregious and the injuries and damages are more serious than what appears on the surface. Furthermore, these million dollar cases are few and far between. They represent a very small minority of all personal injury cases.

Most injury cases are resolved for amounts that are much less than a million dollars and many times for much less than six figures, including cases involving severe injuries. Many severe injuries receive inadequate or no compensation at all due to a variety of factors, not the least of which is the vigorous defense often mounted by the insurance company either to defeat the case entirely or to significantly decrease the value of the claim. The insurance carrier does this by hiring aggressive defense attorneys and high-priced experts to say that the accident was someone else's fault, that the injuries were not severe, or that they were caused by some other factor or pre-existing condition. Most people have no idea about the extreme efforts some insurance carriers will make to defeat even legitimate claims. It is not uncommon for companies to spend much more money defending the claim by hiring lawyers and experts than what they would spend to settle the case for a reasonable sum. The carrier does this to dissuade other potential claimants and their lawyers from pursuing claims.

The insurance industry's far-reaching propaganda machine has created the false impression in the public's mind that the system needs to be fixed. Unfortunately, this campaign to spread disinformation has had an enormous negative influence on juries and their verdicts. Juries today are highly skeptical of people who file lawsuits that claim money for "pain and suffering," even when those claims involve children. Many people who end up on juries believe the myths touted by the insurance industry. They may be persuaded by the arguments of the insurance carrier's high-priced attorneys and the testimony of their formidable experts who earn substantial income working for the defense. Since the existence of an insurance policy as a means of compensating a victim is never admissible in court, the task of securing a just and fair award from a jury may be especially difficult. These efforts by the industry may be a huge obstacle to achieving justice in your case, even when the injuries are severe and the negligence of the other party has been conclusively established. Lawyers who handle injury cases have learned that it is difficult to achieve justice for their clients in today's climate of skepticism and heightened propaganda.

If you have an injury claim, you need to be aware that the insurance adjustor will use any means necessary to pay out as little as possible, even on legitimate claims that involve serious injuries. It does not matter to the adjustor that the injuries are so catastrophic that they evoke tremendous sympathy. Insurance claims adjustors receive extensive training on how to save the company money, rather than how to examine a claim fairly and pay victims a reasonable settlement. In fact, most insurance companies reward their claims adjustors with bonuses or promotions based on how much money these adjustors save the company, rather than on whether the claims are settled fairly. So, when the adjustor listens to the facts of your injury claim, he or she is thinking of ways to pay out as little as possible so that their bonus is bigger at the end of the year.

Here are some of the tactics the insurance adjustor will use to wear down injured claimants so they will accept much less money than what the claim is worth:

- **Using delay tactics.** Adjustors are masters of using delay tactics to wear people down. They know that many people (80-90%, according to some insurance company estimates) will grow tired of the delay tactics and simply throw up their hands and say, "Enough!" These people will accept low-ball offers just to be done with the entire unpleasant process.

- **Requesting unnecessary information.** It is true that the insurance company will need records, receipts, bills, reports, and other documentation to support the claim, but sometimes the requests for documentation are unnecessary—for example, asking for medical records from ten years before the accident or asking for tax returns from the same period. Such information typically is unnecessary and is being requested only to delay resolution of the claim. Insurance adjustors know that repeated requests for unnecessary documentation can easily frustrate people and wear them down so that they are more likely to accept low settlement offers.

- **Disputing the medical treatment.** Despite the absence of any medical training, insurance adjustors may question the need for certain treatments or procedures, or worse—second-guess your own doctor. Many times it does not matter to the adjustor that your treatment has been recommended by a reputable, licensed physician.

- **Disputing the medical charges.** Sometimes the adjustor will only agree to "accept" 70, 80, or 90% of your past medical charges. Again, such an assertion is made without any medical background to support such a position. By nickel-and-diming the consumer, the well-trained adjustor knows that most people will be worn down, and will not hire a lawyer to challenge the refusal to pay a small portion of the medical bills.

- **Telling you not to hire an attorney.** Other times, the insurance company will tell you that hiring an attorney is unnecessary. Sometimes the adjustor will try to prevent you from retaining an attorney by falsely stating that any settlement money you receive will go entirely to the attorney. Still other times, the adjustor may threaten to "deny" the claim if you hire a lawyer. If a claims representative tries to steer you away from retaining an attorney, this should be your first clue that using an attorney may actually produce a much higher recovery for you–even after deducting the attorney's fee.

- **Misrepresenting insurance policy benefits.** Sometimes the adjustor will misrepresent the amount of insurance coverage that is available to you. Worse, the adjustor won't tell you that the insurance coverage or certain types of benefits even exist. This tactic may be used to entice you into accepting a smaller settlement than what would otherwise be warranted.

- **Acting as your friend.** There are times when the claims adjustor will "befriend" you and make it appear that he is watching out for your interests when in fact that is not the case. Sometimes the adjustor will give you advice about the type or frequency of your medical treatment, and then decide later on not to pay for the treatment because it is "excessive."

- **Making false promises.** There are times when the adjustor will make promises to you that she knows can't be met. The adjustor's primary loyalty is to his or her employer (the insurance company) and to his or her insured (the negligent party). Any adjustor who makes promises "for your benefit" inherently creates a conflict of interest. Oftentimes the adjustor already knows that a conflict is created by promising to protect your interests, but she knows this is one way to get you to lower your guard and get you to agree to terms that your attorney would never allow.

These are just a few of the tactics that the insurance industry will use to accomplish its goal of getting people to accept smaller settlements. You need to be aware that you are dealing with professional negotiators who strive to fulfill the insurance company's primary objective: to settle claims for much less than they are worth. Lower settlements mean bigger company profits. If you begin to feel overwhelmed, you should not hesitate to consult with an attorney,

The Claims Process

The insurance claims process is intimidating and stressful. So is the process of negotiating and settling a serious bicycle injury case without a deep understanding of the law and your legal rights. Insurance companies as a whole aggressively resist or defend personal injury cases to avoid paying out a reasonable settlement or verdict. Like most businesses, insurance companies are focused primarily on increasing profits for their sharcholders. Unfortunately, one of the primary targets of their cost-cutting measures is you—the person who brings a claim. In a bicycle injury case, the insurance adjustor assigned to your case may try to settle the claim fast and at a relatively low dollar figure before you have a true understanding of your injuries, damages, and what the claim may generally be worth. What may seem like a large sum of money at first can later be judged as deceptively low; especially if you are facing expenses for hospitalization, surgery, and prolonged treatment and rehabilitation. Sometimes, the adjustor will try to settle quickly in order to dissuade you from hiring an attorney. This occurs because the insurance company knows that an experienced personal injury attorney will likely have better leverage when negotiating a case and can recover much more money than you can recover on your own.

Unfortunately, I see the flat-out denial of legitimate claims in my practice, as more insurance companies are looking for any reason they can find in order to deny a claim. Sometimes, the insurance adjustor may misrepresent the amount of insurance coverage that is available. Other times, the insurance company may falsely represent which parties may be legally at fault and therefore liable for paying monetary damages. Sometimes, the carrier may give false legal advice about the status of the personal injury laws, or misrepresent the type and/or quantity of damages that may be recoverable. Whatever the reason or method used to defeat a claim, you may be the victim of an overzealous insurance company that is focused on increasing its profits.

The insurance company cannot be trusted to protect your interests. No matter how compassionate and caring the claims representative may seem, keep in mind that the insurance company's interests and your interests are always adverse. That typically means that the carrier loses when you recover a fair and reasonable settlement for your claim.

Filing a Claim

How do you file a claim in a bicycle injury case? The very first step is to call your insurance carrier and report the claim. You may also want to contact the at-fault person's insurance company to report the claim. But do not give too much information and never give a recorded statement to the at-fault carrier. You should, however, be prepared to give some basic facts about what has occurred: where, when, and how. Please remember that most of the information needed initially by the carrier will be contained in the police report. You may wish to get a copy of the report before discussing the details of the claim with the at-fault driver's insurance carrier.

You may also wish to delay talking to the other person's insurance adjustor about the specifics of the claim until the initial shock of the accident has worn off. I have seen insurance adjustors use a victim's shock to the advantage of the insurance company. If you are distraught and overwhelmed by your or a loved one's injuries, you may say or do things that could impact the claim in the future. Statements you make about what happened in the accident can be used against you later if a personal injury case is filed. Keep in mind that just because an insurance company representative calls you does not mean you are obligated to speak with them. Your only obligation is to protect yourself and your family during this difficult time.

Speaking with the Insurance Claims Adjustor

By pursuing a personal injury claim, you will likely be interviewed by a claims representative from your own insurance company, the at-fault person's insurance company, or both. You might think the adjustor is trying to help you, especially if it is the adjustor from your own insurance company. Do not be surprised to discover that this may not be the case at all. Each insurance company adjustor owes their allegiance and concern to her employer, not to you. Be aware that your interests and the insurance company's interests almost always oppose each other. You want the carrier to pay as much money as possible to resolve the claim, while the insurance company wants to pay out as little as possible. Because these interests are in conflict with each other, consider the following recommendations when talking to any claims representative:

Things to DO When Speaking with an Insurance Adjustor

- **Prepare for the meeting by speaking with your attorney.** Take the time to fully understand the process and make the most of your attorney's expertise and years of experience.

- **Get the basic information.** Before you get started with the interview, write down the name, address, and phone number of the insurance adjustor and insurance company.

- **Give the basic information.** Provide your full name, address, and telephone number to the adjustor.

- **If possible, record the conversation.** If you can't record it, take detailed notes. If you will be recording the conversation, Washington law states that you must get the other person's consent. Since the adjustor will likely be recording the conversation, it would only seem fair that you are permitted to do the same.

- **Find out about witnesses.** Ask the adjustor if he is aware of any witnesses to the accident.

- **Tell the truth.** It is imperative that you are truthful at all times during the interview. Lying or exaggerating can harm the claim.

- **Pause before answering each question.** This will give you time to think about the question and the answer you are about to give. Remember: you are not being timed, so proceed slowly and thoughtfully as you answer each question.

- **Remember that it is okay to answer, "I don't know" or "I don't understand."** Never, ever guess or speculate. Never answer a question you don't understand. Doing so can often cause irreparable damage to the value of your claim.

- **Be cordial.** Treat the adjustor with respect, but be firm and assertive when necessary.

- **Answer "yes" or "no" questions with "yes" or "no."** Not every answer requires follow-up. Try to avoid rambling when answering questions. Often, "yes" or "no" is all you need to say.

Things to AVOID When Speaking with an Insurance Adjustor

- **No recordings.** Do not agree to have the conversation recorded by the insurance adjustor unless your attorney is present on the call.

- **Do not engage in casual conversation.** Insurance adjustors will try to use informal conversation in an effort to relax you and get as many details about the accident as possible. The more detail you give, the greater the chance of creating an inconsistency, which may be used against you later on. Be aware of this.

- **Do not agree to anything.** The call should be about collecting information, NOT about you agreeing to anything.

- **Do not identify witnesses.** During an interview with the adjustor, you are not obligated to identify witnesses or answer every question that is presented to you.

- **Avoid talking in absolutes**. In other words, do not give exact distances, times, or try to calculate the extent of your injuries on your own. Always use qualifying words such as "approximately" when describing the details about the accident. Again, if your "estimate" turns out to be wrong, it will be used to suggest that your testimony is unreliable.

- **Do not give anything except general information.** You should speak with your attorney before you give a formal recorded statement.

- **Keep calm.** Do not argue with or get angry at the adjustor. Acting unprofessional or in a hostile manner can make it much more difficult to obtain a fair settlement of your case.

- **Do not guess at the meaning of any question.** If you do not understand a question, say so. "I don't know" is usually an adequate answer if you don't understand the meaning of the question.

- **Do not volunteer information.** Make sure you fully answer the adjustor's question and then quit speaking. Although it is important to always tell the truth, it is also important not to give more information in your answer than is necessary.

- **Do not interrupt.** When the interviewer is asking the question, allow him to finish even if you think you already know the answer.

- **DO NOT SIGN ANYTHING.** No matter what the insurance adjustor sends to you, never sign anything. Instead, pass the documents along to your attorney for review.

- **Do not answer compound questions with a "yes" or "no" answer.** Compound questions are two or more questions mixed into one. A "yes" or "no" answer may be accurate for one of these questions, but not for the other. Your answer could be misinterpreted.

- **Do not allow the adjustor to assume facts that are not true when asking you a question.** Always be diligent and correct or clarify any untrue statements made by the adjustor.

- **Do not use phrases like "in all honesty" or "I would never lie."** Insurance companies will work hard to get you to contradict yourself after making absolute statements such as this.

- **Do not use words like "always" or "never."** Again, insurance companies look for absolute statements that they can pick apart and use against you during negotiations and jury trials.

- **Do not give long narrative answers.** Short and concise answers are the best.

- **Do not use words like "uh-huh" or "mm-hmm."** These can be misinterpreted or misrepresented, and ultimately change the meaning of your answer.

How Does the Insurance Company Work?

To recover the best settlement, you should know how the insurance company does business. As you already know, the reason any insurance company exists is to make a profit. This is the carrier's primary goal: to make as much money as possible for its executives and shareholders.

Put simply, the insurance company must take in more money than it pays out. There are two primary ways the insurance company will make more money: sell more policies and pay out less in claims. On the claims side, the insurance company will focus on minimizing its liabilities. Any claim is a liability because it means the insurance company will have to pay out money to settle the claim. The insurance claims adjustor's job is to settle a claim for as little as possible, or rejected it altogether. If the adjustor can spot a defense or weakness in your claim, then his or her job is to make sure the weakness is exploited to the fullest extent possible so that it can be used to justify a lower settlement payout.

While the methods used by an insurance company may be ethical in most cases, sometimes they are not. Sometimes an insurance adjustor can actually manufacture a defense by obtaining favorable statements from you and other witnesses. This type of conduct may also include recovering or eliminating favorable evidence that might help your claim. I have handled cases where the carrier has deliberately tried to "lose" evidence that was favorable to my client. Whatever the method used to gather or destroy evidence, just remember that the adjustor is looking for any way to help the company and not you.

To achieve your goal of recovering a fair and reasonable settlement, you must provide the adjustor with strong and compelling reasons that it should pay out more to settle the claim rather than less. This is often accomplished by providing the adjustor with information and documentation to support your claim. There are some pieces of information that may be more persuasive than others. How relevant the information is depends on the facts of the case and the status of the law that applies to the claim. Keep in mind that the more persuasive the evidence submitted to support the claim, the higher the likelihood of a more favorable settlement recovery. Having an experienced attorney working in your corner gives you the absolute best chance of securing a favorable outcome in your case.

Insurance Benefits and Coverage

There are several different types of insurance benefits that may be available to you after an accident. Many people are unaware of the ways that insurance benefits can cover their damages and losses, and the complexity of typical insurance policy documents can make it even more confusing for accident victims. Examples of insurance coverage that may apply to accident claims include:

Funeral benefits

These benefits are available to help surviving loved ones cover the cost of a funeral in the event of a fatal accident. This is typically an optional benefit that may be added on to car insurance policies.

Uninsured Motorist and Underinsured Motorist benefits (UM/UIM)

Uninsured Motorist (UM) coverage applies if the at-fault driver has no insurance. Underinsured Motorist (UIM) coverage applies if the at-fault driver's insurance coverage is insufficient to cover all damages. UIM coverage is a floating layer of coverage; meaning that it is coverage in addition to the coverage held by the at-fault driver. Washington law states that UM/UIM coverage must be offered in the same amount as a driver's liability coverage unless rejected by the insured in writing. If there are multiple policies, then the separate UM/UIM coverage amounts may be stackable unless the policy specifically excludes stacking coverage between separate policies. You should consult an attorney to make this determination.

If you were injured in a bicycle-versus-vehicle accident, then you may have an additional source of coverage as a bicyclist under your own automobile insurance policy. If the at-fault driver was uninsured or underinsured, then your own auto

UM/UIM policy may provide you with the coverage to pay for your damages. You should probably consult with an experienced attorney who can request and review your auto policy to make this determination.

There are different types of insurance policies or types of coverage that may be held by the at-fault party. These coverage types are extremely important because they may often determine whether a personal injury case can be successfully pursued or not.

Personal Insurance Coverage

You should ask for all policies that covered the at-fault party so you can determine if stacking is available. Do not trust the opinions or statements made by the insurance adjustor about what policies exist or may apply. Get the policies and make your own determination, or have an experienced attorney review the policies.

Med Pay

Med Pay is an optional policy added to your auto insurance that covers the immediate and short-term health costs for you and your passengers in the event of a car crash. By covering gaps in regular car and health insurance policies, Med Pay helps to eliminate co-payments and other out-of-pocket medical expenses related to the accident. In the case of a bicycle-auto accident, the bicyclist may be entitled to Med Pay coverage under the other driver's auto policy for the payment of reasonable and necessary medical care received by the bicyclist.

Collision Insurance

If your bicycle is damaged in a collision, various types of collision coverage may compensate you for the damage based on the value of your bicycle and the cost of repairs or replacement.

Personal Injury Protection

Also known as "no-fault insurance," Personal Injury Protection (PIP) is an extension of auto insurance that pays for medical expenses and lost wages and other damages. PIP coverage is similar to Med Pay. Though PIP is mandatory (unless rejected in writing by the driver) in states like Washington, it is sometimes unavailable in others. Like Med Pay coverage, the injured bicyclist may be entitled to the at-fault driver's PIP coverage to pay for reasonable and necessary medical treatment and lost wages caused by the accident. Bicyclists may also be eligible for PIP coverage under their own auto insurance policy.

Umbrella Policies

These are insurance policies that apply when additional coverage is needed to cover the value of the loss. An umbrella policy is also called an "excess policy" because it offers additional coverage on top of a primary policy, like an automobile insurance policy. Many times the existence of an umbrella policy will not be readily known. Umbrella coverage is often purchased by high-net-worth individuals and those who wish to protect their own assets from lawsuits. Sometimes a claims representative will misrepresent whether an umbrella policy exists. If the injuries are serious and there are questions about coverage, it is a good idea to hire an experienced personal injury attorney to investigate whether the at-fault driver has an umbrella policy.

Business Insurance Policies

As the name implies, these are insurance policies that cover the actions of a business entity and that company's employees. A business policy may provide coverage if the at-fault driver was working within the scope of his or her employment when the accident took place. Again, it is usually a good idea to retain counsel if there are questions about whether the driver was working at the time of the accident.

Work Disability

Work disability coverage deals with cases where you are injured and unable to return to your normal employment.

Personal and Business Assets

You may need to look at the personal and business assets of the at-fault party to determine whether they are sufficient to pay the value of the claim if insurance does not exist. If the at-fault party was employed by a major corporation, then the company may be self-insured and also liable for the negligence committed by one of its employees.

During the claims and pre-litigation process, you will want to evaluate the possibility of any other third-party claims. A third-party claim is one that exists against another party who may share some fault for causing the accident that caused your injuries. Some examples of less common third party claims include:

- **Dram shop claims:** If an injury accident is caused by an individual who is intoxicated, such as a drunk driver, then liability may sometimes be imposed on the establishment that served the driver alcohol. Contact an attorney to discuss this very technical and complex area of the law.

- **Employer/employee relationships:** If the at-fault party was acting within the course of her employment when the accident occurred, this may allow for a separate claim against that person's employer.

- **Principal-Agent relationship:** If the at-fault party was acting to further a business or other relationship, the party receiving the benefit of that relationship (called the principal) may also be liable for the wrongful conduct.

- **Governmental liability:** Sometimes a claim may also exist against a local municipality or state agency. For instance, if the at-fault party was operating a motor vehicle and there is evidence to suggest that an unsafe condition of the roadway also contributed to the accident, a claim may exist against the governmental entity responsible for maintaining safe roads. Typically, this type of claim is brought against the State of Washington and/or the particular county where the accident occurred.

Family Car Doctrine

In Washington, a family member (e.g. parent) may be responsible for the at-fault party's actions in a car accident case if the vehicle was owned and/or maintained by a family member of the at-fault person. This situation most commonly arises when the at-fault driver is a young adult and the vehicle has been purchased and/or is maintained by the parent.

How Claims Are Evaluated

Statistically, more than 95% of all bicycle injury claims are settled prior to trial, either during the claims process or during litigation before the trial. A fair and reasonable settlement may be successfully negotiated if your claim is properly documented, presented, and argued to the insurance adjustor. At Davis Law Group, we rely on a number of factors when evaluating a bicycle injury claim. These factors may include:

- **The facts of the accident giving rise to the claim.** If the at-fault party's actions are egregious, the claim may be valued higher than it would have if the acts only amounted to a "simple mistake."

- **Identity of the parties.** If the injury accident was caused by the actions of a sympathetic person (e.g., a grandmother), then the claim may be lower than if the injury accident was caused by an unsympathetic party (e.g., a large multinational corporation).

- **If the bicycle accident was fatal, then the cause of death is important.** The claim may be worth more if the cause of death is uncontested. Similarly, if there are other explanations or prior medical conditions that may have contributed to the person's death, the value of the case may sometimes be lower.

- **Pain and suffering.** In a fatal accident, the value of the claim may be higher if the deceased experienced conscious pain and suffering before death. Typically, the longer the period of time experienced, the higher the value of the claim.

- **Liability defenses.** If the at-fault person can successfully prove that he was not at fault or that someone else was at fault, then the value of the claim might be lowered significantly.

- **Information about the victim.** If there is damaging or embarrassing information about the victim (e.g. he is not a good person, has criminal convictions, or other similar factors), then the value of the claim may be less or the claim could be nonexistent.

- **Existence or lack of insurance coverage.** There must be enough insurance coverage to pay for all of the damages. If the at-fault driver was uninsured you may potentially recover nothing (assuming you have no additional coverage like UM). If the other driver only had minimal coverage, then this may be all that you receive unless additional coverage exists.

- **The experience and reputation of your lawyer.** If you have an experienced lawyer who regularly handles personal injury claims, then this factor may increase the value of your claim in the eyes of the insurance company.

There is no magic formula for placing a value on a person's pain and suffering after an accident–or placing a value on the loss of a person's life. Much of the loss or the amount of damages that are legally recoverable can be purely subjective in nature. Ultimately, the value of any given case is what a jury says it is. No two cases are alike and each one has to be judged on its own merits, given the facts that exist. Because bicycle injury cases are incredibly complex and expensive to pursue, it is often beneficial for victims to consult with an attorney to gain a better understanding of the case value and whether or not hiring a lawyer will improve the chances of a successful outcome.

The Settlement Demand Package

Davis Law Group goes to extraordinary lengths to compile and present effective settlement demand packages to insurance companies. We obtain all documents and materials that may support and prove a claim. We then organize and present the demand package in the most influential and persuasive way possible in an effort to secure the highest settlement recovery.

The settlement demand package may include many different types of documents, records and items, including but not limited to:

- A complete discussion and analysis of the facts of the accident and the laws that may apply.
- Incident reports or police reports.
- Copies of pleadings that are ready to be filed in court in the event that the settlement does not occur (e.g., complaint, deposition notice, etc.).
- Photos of the accident scene or the injuries.
- Medical records and reports.
- Expert reports (e.g., physician, economist, vocational expert, accident reconstructionist, etc.).
- Video re-enactments and/or computer simulations.
- Video testimony from witnesses and/or experts.
- Witness statements.

By providing a comprehensive and persuasive settlement demand package, you are also helping the insurance adjustor build a claim file so that the company can justify paying out a fair settlement. Providing a comprehensive and persuasive settlement demand package gives the insurance company a number of reasons for settling the claim immediately and fairly rather than going to court. Keep in mind that an experienced attorney knows how to present the demand package in an appropriate way so that the information increases the chance of a favorable settlement. A "do it yourself" approach to this step could damage the case and mistakenly provide the insurance company with information that could harm your claim.

Should I Settle or Go to Court?

Your primary goal during the claims process in a bicycle injury accident case is to build your case by collecting and evaluating all evidence that can help you secure a fair and reasonable settlement. Together with an experienced attorney, you will prepare your case as if it is going to go to trial. Even an experienced attorney can never truly know which case will settle and which will go to trial, so it is often important to prepare the case as if it will go all the way to a jury trial.

Avoiding the Risk of Trial

Litigation is risky because juries are always unpredictable. It doesn't matter how strong you think the case may be; a jury can always come up with reasons for a lower verdict or to side with the insurance company about the value of a given case. Going to trial is always going to be a gamble to a certain extent because no one ever knows for sure who will end up on the jury and how each juror will assess and evaluate the evidence that comes in at trial. Therefore, the decision to go to trial must be carefully weighed against the potential risks and costs involved.

Avoiding the Expense of Litigation and Trial

Bicycle injury cases can be very expensive to pursue, especially in those cases where liability is contested or when it's necessary to hire numerous experts to prove the case in court. A single case can incur thousands of dollars in expenses. Sometimes the total expense of a trial can easily exceed six figures. Attorney ethics rules require that the expense of litigation must always be borne by the client, though the attorney may advance these costs and then get reimbursed at the conclusion of the case. Usually the expenses of litigation will include the cost of hiring a number of experts, paying for depositions, performing other discovery, requesting numerous records, and creating trial exhibits. The litigation process can also affect your income as you or family members may have to take time off work to attend a deposition and/or sit through trial.

The disadvantage of settling your claim is that you will never know how a jury would have viewed the case and how much the verdict would have been. Many times it comes down to whether or not you want to take the risk of going to trial. At some point, you should have a very candid conversation with your attorney about your expectations and the estimated value of the case. The pros and cons of litigation must be carefully weighed so that you can make the best decision for yourself and your family. Since each case is different and may involve different legal questions, your decision must be based on the specific facts involved.

Chapter Eight: The Litigation Process

A Word of Caution

The laws and procedures governing bicycle injury claims can be complex. The same holds true for the litigation process in an injury case, since the rules governing litigation are often entirely dependent on the laws and procedures in the local jurisdiction — the area where the case will be tried. That is why it is extremely important that you consult with a local attorney who has experience litigating personal injury cases. This section is only intended to provide a general overview of the litigation process for the personal injury case in the state of Washington and should not be taken as a substitute for professional legal advice provided by an attorney.

Pre-litigation Investigation

It is impossible to ignore or understate the importance of conducting an investigation before a lawsuit begins. Oftentimes, obtaining evidence well before the lawsuit is filed can drastically improve the chances of a successful outcome in the personal injury case. For instance, it is usually wise to obtain witness statements as soon as possible. Taking measurements at the scene may also be important since certain evidence like skid marks, debris, etc. can disappear within days. Most experienced personal injury attorneys will want to conduct some pre-litigation investigation before filing a lawsuit unless the attorney is retained a long time after the accident or if there are time limits imposed (e.g., a pending statute of limitations).

Filing a Lawsuit

To file a personal injury lawsuit, a number of documents, called pleadings, are filed with the court along with a fee paid to the court clerk. In Washington, these pleadings are called the summons and complaint. The summons informs the person being sued that a lawsuit is being filed and that the person must respond to the lawsuit within a certain period of time. The deadline for Washington residents is 20 days from the date of receiving the papers and 60 days for non-residents. The complaint sets forth the facts that support the claim along with a description or statement of the legal theories that are being alleged against the wrongdoer. The personal injury complaint will usually identify the parties, the facts or circumstances involved in the accident and the specific laws that support or authorize the personal injury cause of action.

The person who files a personal injury lawsuit is called the plaintiff (often referred to here as the injured party or the claimant.) The person or party that is being sued is called the defendant. Usually the plaintiff must arrange to personally serve a copy of the summons and complaint on each defendant. The lawsuit is usually divided up into different stages, which include:

1. Pre-litigation and information-gathering
2. Pre-trial discovery (e.g. depositions, interrogatories, etc.)
3. Pre-trial settlement or alternative dispute resolution
4. Trial
5. Post-trial or appellate process

The length of time for each of these phases will depend on the complexity of the case as well as the laws and rules of the local jurisdiction where the case is being litigated.

The Discovery Process

After the personal injury lawsuit is filed and the defendant is properly served in a timely way, both sides participate in a process of exchanging information about the case. This process is known as discovery. There are many different forms of discovery or different ways to request or obtain information from the other side in a case. In Washington, the rules governing the discovery process are quite broad and allow each side to investigate what evidence and witnesses may be introduced at trial. Even if the requested information does not appear directly relevant to the case, it may still be a proper request if it could lead to the discovery of relevant information. One form of discovery may involve sending or answering written questions called interrogatories. There may also be written requests for production of documents and other materials that are relevant to the claims being made in the suit. There may be limits to the number of written questions or requests that can be exchanged, depending on the local court rules. When the interrogatories and requests for production are answered and completed, you must also execute a document stating that the answers and responses are true and accurate.

Another form of discovery may include a deposition. This is a face-to-face meeting where the attorneys are allowed to ask witnesses questions under oath while a court reporter transcribes the session. Any witness who may offer testimony at trial can be deposed: yourself, your doctor, the medical examiner or coroner, other family members, eyewitnesses, and experts involved in the case. The deposition is a very important legal proceeding that should almost always involve preparation by the personal injury attorney and the person who is going to be deposed. A person's performance at their deposition can have a huge influence on the success or value of the personal injury case, usually because these individuals are very important in communicating and establishing the extent of the losses caused by the personal injury.

In addition to interrogatories, requests for production, and depositions, each side's lawyer may also be permitted to issue a subpoena. This is a request to produce documents or items in addition to requesting that the person appear at a deposition or trial. For instance, the personal injury attorney may wish to subpoena the medical examiner's records for documents. Financial, employment, and medical records may be requested by subpoena to help establish various elements or issues involved in the case.

The discovery phase may also include a request by the other side that the plaintiff must submit to a medical examination and/or a psychological evaluation. Washington's discovery rules permit one party to request such an exam or evaluation for the purpose of learning more about the person's health and to evaluate the person's claim for damages. The legal and factual grounds necessary to support a request to conduct a medical examination or psychological evaluation on the plaintiff will depend on the facts of the case and the issues involved. In most cases, the judge will have considerable discretion to grant or deny the defendant's request for a medical or psychological evaluation on a case-by-case basis.

Using Expert Witnesses

After a personal injury case has been filed in court, it will often require the assistance of expert testimony to help the attorney prove one or more elements of the cause of action. Since personal injury cases can involve many different issues that are often complex and difficult to prove, an experienced personal injury attorney will usually want to engage the assistance of one or more experts early on in the case.
Sometimes, the success of a personal injury case will hinge on the credibility and/or knowledge of the experts involved. This is why it is extremely important that the attorney have substantial experience in handling personal injury cases as well as having the knowledge of the different types of experts that may be necessary to achieve a successful result.

There are many different types of experts that can be used in a personal injury action. Generally, experts can fall into two classifications in the personal injury case:

- Liability experts
- Damage experts

Liability Experts

Certain experts may be necessary to help prove that the defendant was responsible for the incident that caused the plaintiff's injury or death. There are numerous examples of different types of experts who may help prove the defendant's liability or negligence. Usually, the person's field of expertise will depend on the circumstances that led to the accident. Examples of liability experts may include those in the fields of accident reconstruction, engineering, bio-mechanical engineering, medicine, physics, or metallurgy.

Take the case of an automobile/pedestrian accident that caused another person's death. If there is a dispute about who caused the accident, the personal injury attorney may wish to hire an accident reconstruction expert to review the facts and circumstances of the collision and then offer an expert opinion about exactly how the accident occurred. This expert will usually want to visit the scene of the accident, take measurements and photographs, and collect any other evidence to help determine how the accident happened.

Damages Experts

One frequent reason for the use of experts in a personal injury case is to address the issue of damages. There may be several different types or classification of damages that may be sought in the personal injury case depending on the facts of the case and the legal issues involved. An experienced personal injury lawyer will hire the best experts to help uncover and explain certain evidence, which in turn increases the likelihood of a successful result. Generally, the classification of damages experts may fall into two categories: economic damage experts and non-economic damage experts.

"Economic damages" are hard or tangible damages that are usually easier to calculate, like lost wages, medical expenses, future income loss, or other assets. Examples of economic damage experts include economists, medical experts, accountants, vocational experts, and life care planners.

One of the most common types of damages requested in a personal injury case is a claim for future lost earnings or the future net lost accumulations of assets. A vocational expert may be necessary to help establish your lost income and/or future occupational advancement opportunities. An economist or accountant may be necessary to calculate the present value of the future lost earnings based on your occupation, anticipated future promotions, and your savings and consumption rate.

When using experts to calculate economic damages, it is often important to involve the expert early on in the case and it is also important to furnish the expert with all of the necessary documentation required for her to form an opinion. For instance, when calculating future lost earnings, the expert may need to review several different types of records involving employment, tax, educational, medical, bank, insurance, or other financial documents.

The second category of damages consists of "non-economic damages" and refers to those subjective or intangible losses that are usually more difficult to quantify. They include pain and suffering. Thus, it is often wise to retain one or more experts to address these types of damages to a jury.

Take the case involving the serious personal injury or death of a child. The parents in this case will likely suffer a substantial amount of psychological distress and suffering. In this situation, it may be beneficial to use a psychological expert, like a psychiatrist, psychologist, or mental health therapist, to discuss the parents' loss of their child. There may be long-term emotional issues that surviving parents and children may face as a result of losing a loved one prematurely. Thus, using an expert to discuss, explain, and highlight these losses may be very helpful to explaining the parents' loss to the jury.

Another category of damages in the event of a fatal accident may include pain and suffering. Remember that Washington law permits the estate to recover damages for pre-death pain and suffering. If there is a dispute over whether the deceased did experience pain or fear right before death, then a medical or psychological expert may be useful to establish this fact.

Oftentimes, the choice of an expert is a very important factor that can have a huge influence on the success of the personal injury case. Sometimes, the distinguished academic and professional credentials of the expert are extremely important. Other times, the ability of the expert to teach and explain the particular field of expertise to a jury or lay person may be valued more highly than the particular expert's academic credentials or success. Choosing which particular expert will work best is usually a judgment call by the personal injury attorney and should be based on the specific needs of the case.

Personal injury attorneys must also be mindful of the expense of hiring and using experts, which can be considerable and cost many thousands of dollars. There has to be a real need for the expert in order to engage one for a case. The economics of the case must also justify the expense of using experts. Above all else, the attorney must choose experts carefully and use them only to highlight or explain certain issues in the case. Sometimes, there may only be a few qualified well-regarded experts in a particular field of study, so an experienced personal injury attorney may wish to retain one or more of these experts immediately, before the defense attorney can do so.

Again, the unique facts and circumstances of the case will often dictate which type of expert to use and how many experts will be necessary in the case. Because experts are a critical component in a successful personal injury case, it is usually beneficial to retain an experienced personal injury attorney early on so there is sufficient time to locate, hire, and brief each expert who may be necessary to support the merits of the case.

Alternative Dispute Resolution or Mediation

Depending on the jurisdiction and the complexity of a personal injury case, the discovery phase in litigation may take many months or sometimes even years. When discovery is finally completed, and each side generally knows what evidence will likely be offered at trial, the parties may then begin to conduct settlement discussions. Sometimes, the law of the particular jurisdiction or venue will require that the parties engage in meaningful efforts to settle the case other than just simply negotiating between themselves. These efforts are sometimes called alternative dispute resolution or ADR. One example of ADR is mediation. In mediation, the parties agree to hire an impartial person called the mediator to help them settle the case. Oftentimes, the mediator is a retired judge or an experienced attorney who has advanced training and/or education in the area of ADR.

Usually, the process of mediation is voluntary and non-binding unless a settlement is reached. This means that a mediator cannot force a party to settle and either party is permitted to reject offers from the other side. But the parties are expected to participate in mediation in good faith with the goal of trying to settle the case instead of going to trial. Typically, the mediator goes back and forth between the parties and communicates settlement offers. The mediator may also communicate strengths and weaknesses of each side's case and discuss potential outcomes if the case proceeds to trial.

A mediation session is typically a confidential proceeding, so anything that is said during the session cannot be used at trial. Many times, mediation can be used successfully to resolve a case involving personal injury claims. Mediation sessions can be held over the course of one day or over several days, depending on the size and complexity of the case.

Evaluating settlement offers at mediation or during ADR depends on many factors. The experience of the personal injury attorney is often important because a settlement offer will always be judged in relation to how a jury may decide the case. Thus, you want an attorney who has successfully litigated personal injury cases in the past. Both sides will attempt to predict how a jury might rule and then factor this into their evaluation of the case. The specific facts involved in the case and how those factors are highlighted or proved by the personal injury attorney can also have an enormous influence on the insurance company's evaluation of the case.

Preparing for Trial

If the case does not settle after discovery and ADR or mediation has failed, then the case may proceed to trial. Each side has the option of trying the case before a judge or jury. Depending on the jurisdiction, a jury trial may not happen automatically. One party may have to specifically request that the case be decided by a jury as opposed to a judge. In most personal injury cases, the defense attorney will request a jury trial by filing a document in court called a jury demand and then paying a jury fee to the clerk. In Washington, the court rules usually require that certain documents must be filed and exchanged within 30 to 90 days before the trial date. These documents may include each side's witness and exhibits list, pre-trial motions, objections to evidence or trial exhibits, trial memorandums, and jury instructions, among others.

Going to trial in a personal injury case usually requires a tremendous amount of resources, time, and preparation. The personal injury attorney usually has to invest a substantial amount of money and time in the case to conduct depositions, hire and prepare experts, create trial exhibits, and draft and prepare the necessary documents that must be filed in court. The insurance companies and their attorneys know how expensive and time-consuming a personal injury case is to pursue. As a result, they may use this fact to their advantage by intentionally delaying resolution of the case over a long period of time.

Understandably, most people want to avoid going to trial. A trial is stressful and can cause additional anxiety for everyone involved. Usually a trial is the last resort to resolve a claim. Oftentimes, the insurance company will not want a serious or significant personal injury case to go to trial, particularly when there is no serious dispute about the defendant's negligence and the cause of death. However, some insurance companies have a reputation for utilizing scorched-earth litigation tactics, which means needlessly forcing and prolonging the litigation process in an effort to wear down the personal injury attorney and the family so that they will accept a smaller settlement. Sometimes, this will include forcing an unnecessary trial, especially if the insurance company is convinced that the personal injury attorney has little experience in trying injury cases in court.

Oftentimes, a personal injury attorney can secure a reasonable and favorable settlement offer only by threatening and preparing for trial. This is usually why it is extremely important that any personal injury claim be handled by an attorney who has experience with personal injury cases. You don't want to hire a lawyer for a personal injury case only to find out a few weeks or months before trial that the lawyer has limited experience handling personal injury cases or has never tried a significant case in court. In those situations, it may be too late to hire another attorney to take over the case.

Children Testifying in Court

If a lawsuit has been filed to recover financial compensation for a child's injuries, then that child may be called to testify in court. However, most cases involving children never go to court. In my experience representing injured children, the chances that a child will actually be forced to testify in court are extremely low.

The age of the child does not necessarily determine whether a child can or should testify. In Washington, the admission of testimony by children under age ten is within the discretion of the trial court.[29] Children under age ten who appear incapable of understanding the subject matter or facts, or incapable of communicating information, may not be considered competent to testify.[30]

Generally, a child may be held competent to testify if that child:

1. Understands the obligation to speak the truth on the witness stand.
2. Has the mental capacity, at the time of the occurrence concerning which the child is to testify, to receive an accurate impression of it.
3. Has a memory sufficient to retain an independent recollection of the occurrence.
4. Has the capacity to express in words a memory of the occurrence.
5. Has the capacity to understand simple questions about the occurrence.

---

29. Lauderinilk v. Caipenter, 78 Wn.2d92, 102,457 P.2d 1004 (1969)
30. 30 RCW5.60.050(2)

The final determination of whether the child is competent to testify will rest with the judge, who will evaluate and listen to the child, as well as consider the child's demeanor and manner of testifying.

Likelihood of Going to Court

Most personal injury cases settle without going to court or trial. Statistically speaking, the chance that a typical personal injury case will go to trial is extremely small, probably less than five percent of all cases. The likelihood that a personal injury case involving a minor child will go to court is probably even smaller. In cases where the evidence of liability against the defendant is strong and the injuries are fairly serious, the likelihood of the case going to court will be even smaller.

Despite the low probability of a personal injury case ever going to court, the case should still be thoroughly prepared as if it were going to trial. Insurance companies and their attorneys will not agree to pay a premium settlement offer unless they are convinced that there is a strong possibility of a jury awarding much more money if the case were to go to trial. A case that has been competently and thoroughly prepared will therefore increase the likelihood that the case will settle before trial.

Chapter Nine: The Advantages of Hiring a Lawyer

If you have suffered injuries caused by a bicycle accident, you may want to hire an experienced attorney who has years of experience dealing with insurance companies to protect your interests. Remember, the insurance company will be doing everything it can to minimize the claim and avoid paying fair compensation to cover the injured person's past expenses, damages, and future needs. Don't help the adjustor by going it alone. Please give serious thought to hiring an experienced attorney to handle your personal injury claim, especially when the injuries are serious or permanent or when they involve significant scarring or disfigurement.

Is a Lawyer Always Necessary?

Not every case requires a lawyer. In fact, most cases do not. How do you know if a lawyer is necessary for your case? There are no hard and fast rules about the decision to hire an attorney, but generally speaking, the damages should be high enough to justify the expense of hiring a lawyer. We refer to this evaluation as the "economics of the claim." For example, if a lawyer believes your claim is worth $20,000, but will cost $30,000 in litigation expenses and attorney fees to pursue, then the claim is not economically viable. In most cases where the injuries are long lasting or permanent, and the medical bills exceed $10,000 to $20,000 then it may make sense to hire a professional to represent your interests and settle the claim for maximum value.

What Is a Serious Personal Injury that May Justify Hiring a Lawyer?

Again, there are no hard and fast rules. Recovering from a serious personal injury can require several thousands of dollars in past and future medical expense, but I have also seen serious personal injury injuries when the total medical charges are low, yet the injury leaves significant or permanent scarring and disfigurement. In the latter type of case, a significant scar injury, especially one to the victim's face, can command a settlement figure well into the high five figures or low six figures.

In personal injury cases involving children, a lawyer may be advisable. When the child has received permanent scars and/or disfigurement, I usually recommend that the parents hire an experienced attorney. There are other legal requirements involved in child injury claims that will usually justify the involvement of an attorney.

When it comes to making a decision about hiring a lawyer, accident victims should remember that each case is different and the decision to hire counsel will depend on the individual facts involved. When in doubt, a personal injury victim should at least consult with an experienced lawyer to learn more about his or her legal rights and to determine whether hiring an attorney is the best decision. Most reputable attorneys will be upfront about whether a particular case is too small to justify the expense of a lawyer. And since most personal injury lawyers work on a contingency fee basis, there is typically no obligation to meeting with an attorney to discuss the legal options available.

What Is a Contingency Fee?

Understandably, most people are wary of hiring an attorney because of the expense. Cases involving injury claims, including those involving personal injuries, are usually handled by experienced lawyers on a contingency basis. With a contingent fee agreement, the lawyer agrees to defer legal fees until the case successfully resolves. The fee is based on a percentage of the recovery obtained by the lawyer. If there is no recovery, then no attorney fee is owed. Most contingency fees can range anywhere from one-third to 50% of the recovery, depending on the complexity and/or difficulty of the case. Usually, the customary contingency fee rate is around one-third of the settlement or recovery obtained by the lawyer.

Often a serious personal injury case can take years to resolve and the lawyer will spend hundreds of hours on the case before getting paid. The riskier and more complex the case, the higher the contingency fee will usually be. If a lawyer takes on a case that has a high risk of failure, and hence the possibility of receiving no fee, that lawyer will usually want a higher contingency fee as a premium for taking on this risk.

Contingency fees allow people of limited financial resources to hire the best legal representation possible. This helps to level the playing field because the insurance company will usually retain some of the most expensive and experienced defense attorneys to help deny, delay, or defend the claim.

The costs associated with a claim are a different matter. The term "costs" refers to those expenses that are incurred while investigating the claim and if necessary, litigating the case in court. Examples of typical costs include expert fees, court costs, deposition fees, and record retrieval expenses. In Washington, an attorney is permitted to advance all costs and then deduct them from the client's recovery at the conclusion of the case. This allows the client to hire an attorney without ever having to pay out of pocket. Most experienced and reputable accident attorneys will agree to advance costs in a case. There are exceptions, of course, depending on the type of case and the facts involved.

What a Quality Lawyer Can Do For You

Many people do not know what an experienced lawyer can do in these types of cases. I can't speak for every personal injury attorney, but here is a list of the types of services that my office will often provide to our clients:

- Conduct an initial interview with you.
- Educate and teach you about the claims process.
- Educate and teach parents and/or children about the court approval and *Settlement Guardian ad Litem* process (in cases involving injured children).
- Educate you about the litigation process.
- Draft and file petition to appoint the Settlement *Guardian ad Litem* (SGAL) (in those cases involving children).
- Gather written records and documents to support the claim; including medical records, school records, police report, etc.
- Perform investigation of your claim, including gathering witness statements, photographs, diagrams, and physical evidence.
- Read and analyze applicable insurance policies that may apply (e.g., auto, homeowners, health) to see what coverage is available to pay for your damages, like medical, hospital, and wage loss benefits.
- Meet and confer with your medical doctors and other health care providers to fully understand your condition.
- Meet and confer with the SGAL to discuss the case and provide all relevant information regarding the child's claim (in cases involving children).
- Obtain specific reports from experts to support your claim.
- Analyze any pertinent legal issues that may affect your case, such as contributory negligence, assumption of

risk, comparative fault, etc.

- File necessary claim forms with the at-fault governmental agency.
- Arrange for personal service of the summons and your case, such as the personal injury statute, common law complaint on the defendant as required by law.
- Analyze your health insurance or governmental benefit plan to determine whether any money spent by either entity on behalf of the victim must be repaid.
- Analyze and address any liens asserted against the settlement recovery.
- Assist you in locating available resources to help with your recovery (local, state, federal, and nonprofit assistance programs).
- Contact the insurance company and conduct periodic discussions with the carrier about the case so that appropriate reserves are set aside to settle it.
- Conduct negotiations with the insurance adjustor in an effort to settle the claim, either prior to litigation or trial.
- If a lawsuit is to be filed, prepare and draft the summons and complaint to file in court.
- Perform an investigation to locate the defendant so that personal service of the summons and complaint can be achieved.
- Arrange for personal service of the summons and complaint of the defendant as required by law.
- Prepare and draft written questions for information from the other side. These are called *interrogatories* and *requests for production.*
- Prepare you for a deposition.
- Prepare for and conduct the deposition of the defendant and other lay witnesses.
- Meet with your physicians and prepare for their own deposition when requested by the defense attorney.

- Prepare for the deposition of the defendant's experts; including medical experts.
- Answer questions and produce information and records requested by the other side.
- Review and analyze your medical records and billings.
- Hire other necessary experts to support or prove the claim; including other physicians, economists, engineers, vocational experts, etc.
- Review and analyze expert reports about the case; including those addressing liability, injuries, and damages.
- File the necessary documents in court as required by the judge, including witness list, trial readiness, settlement conferences, etc.
- Prepare you and other witnesses for trial.
- Create and prepare exhibits for trial.
- Organize records and other documentary evidence intended to be introduced at trial.
- Prepare for mediation and/or arbitration by organizing records and other documents for submission to the mediator or arbitrator.
- Research and write briefs and file motions to keep out or let in certain evidence at trial.
- Perform or participate in mock trial or focus groups to prepare for trial.
- Try the case over the course of several days before a judge or jury.
- Analyze the verdict and research any issues that occurred at the trial.
- Write briefs or motions following the verdict to obtain post-trial relief, including motion for attorney fees, or to overturn the verdict.
- Analyze trial record to determine if an appeal is warranted.

- Research and write briefs and motions if an appeal is filed.
- Negotiate subrogation claims submitted by a third-party (the insurance company, or a government agency) that the has the right to be paid back out of the settlement recovery from benefits previously paid to or on behalf of you.
- Review and analyze the SGAL's report regarding the recommendation to approve or reject the child's settlement (in those cases involving children).
- Draft and prepare the petition asking the court to approve the settlement.
- If a blocked account is to be open for you, provide the financial institution with necessary information.
- If an annuity is to be purchased, provide the furnisher of that annuity with all necessary information and complete all necessary paperwork, release forms, the disclosure statement, etc.
- If a trust form is to be created for the benefit of a child, review and complete all necessary paperwork, release forms, disclosure statements, etc. (in those cases involving children).
- Draft and file in court the appropriate written proof or receipts showing creation of a blocked account, annuity purchase, or managed trust account.

This is a general list of various tasks that the lawyer may need to complete in any given case. There may be additional tasks, depending on the facts of the case. This list will at least give you some idea of the type of work that may be necessary to successfully pursue a legal claim on your behalf.

Chapter Ten: Important Resources

Cycling is an increasing part of our everyday lives. Not only is cycling part of a healthy lifestyle, but it also saves energy and provides a greener alternative to motor vehicles. However, bicycle accidents often result in serious injuries and even death. They can result in a lifetime of pain, a diminished lifestyle, or the loss of a loved one. If such tragedies are to be avoided, then what is required is to support organizations and programs dedicated to making our roads safer for everyone. Everyone, cyclists and motorists, should educate themselves about the issues, how to improve safety, and understand their rights and duties.

For further information, check out these websites:

Bicycle resources

League of American Bicyclists
(*Bikeleague.org*)
Advocacy group promoting bicycle rights and safety on the local and national level.

Bicycle Club Cascade
(*Bttp://www.cascade.org*)
Seattle-based 13,000-member non-profit cycling organization dedicated to creating a better community through bicycling.

Bicycle Helmet Safety Institute
(*Bhsi.org*)
National organization that provides education on the importance of bicycle helmets, how to choose a helmet, and teaching kids to ride safely.

Bicyclesafe.com
(Bicyclesafe.com)
Resource site with lots of safety advice as well as examples of successful pro-bicycle safety lawsuits against municipalities.

Pedestrian and Bicycle Information Center
(Bicyclinginfo.org)
Bicycle advocacy group with advice on organizing community action.

Bike Smart
(Seattle.gov/transportation/bikesmart.htm)
Bicycle education page from the Seattle city government

Bicycle Alliance of Seattle
(Bicyclealliance.org)
Advocacy group dedicated to increasing bicycle ridership, infrastructure, legislation, and education.

Alliance for Biking and Walking
(Peoplepoweredmovement.org)
North American coalition of grassroots bicycle and pedestrian advocacy organizations.

BicycleTutor.com
(Bicycletutor.com)
Bicycle education resource site with lots of online tutorials.

BikeWise
(Bikewise.org)
Site dedicated to bicycle crashes, hazards, and thefts.

About the Author

Washington attorney Christopher Michael Davis has been representing individuals in accident cases and against insurance companies since 1994. In 2006, he was named a Rising Star Attorney by Washington Law & Politics magazine (this recognition is given only to the top 2.5% of lawyers age 40 and under in Washington State). In 2007, Washington Law & Politics named Mr. Davis a Super Lawyer (the top 5% of lawyers in Washington). Mr. Davis speaks at Continuing Legal Education seminars on topics related to personal injury. He teaches and instructs other lawyers in Washington State on topics such as jury selection, proving damages and developing winning trial techniques. Mr. Davis has been licensed to practice law in Washington State since 1993. He has obtained millions of dollars in verdicts and settlements for his clients. Mr. Davis is a member of numerous professional organizations, including the Washington State Trial Lawyers Association, American Association for Justice, and the North American Brain Injury Society. For a sampling of verdicts and settlements achieved by Mr. Davis in a variety of cases, please visit DavisLawGroupSeattle.com.

Washington Accident Books is a free service provided by

Davis Law Group, P.S.
2101 4th Ave
Suite 1030
Seattle, WA 98121

Do you have a question about a personal injury or wrongful death case? Our legal team may be able to help.

Phone: (206) 727-4000
Email: info@injurytriallawyer.com
Website: DavisLawGroupSeattle.com